ACCA

Performance Management (PM)

Pocket Notes

British library cataloguing-in-publication data

A catalogue record for this book is available from the British Library.

Published by:
Kaplan Publishing UK
Unit 2 The Business Centre
Molly Millars Lane
Wokingham
Berkshire
RG41 2QZ

ISBN 978-1-83996-420-6

© Kaplan Financial Limited, 2023

Printed and bound in Great Britain.

Contents

The exam

Section A of the examination comprises 15 objective test questions (OT) of 2 marks each. Section B comprises three objective test cases (OT cases), each of which includes 5 OT questions of 2 marks each. Section C comprises two 20 marks constructed response (i.e. long) questions.

There will be an even mixture of written requirements and computational requirements. The Section A and Section B questions can cover any area of the syllabus.

The two 20 mark questions in Section C will test decision-making techniques, budgeting and control and/or performance measurement and control areas of the syllabus.

The examiner's key concerns

- Students need to be able to interpret any numbers they calculate and see the limitations of their financial analysis.

- In particular financial performance indicators may give a limited perspective and NFPIs are often needed to see the full picture.

- Questions will be practical and realistic, so will not dwell on unnecessary academic complications.

- Many questions will be designed so discussion aspects can be attempted even if students have struggled with calculation aspects.

Exam technique

Time management

A common problem on this type of paper is that students spend too long on calculations and don't have enough time to do themselves justice on the discussion aspects. Allocate your time and stick to it!

Question requirements and answer content

Ensure you read each question requirement at least twice before you start, and again when you have finished answering it. Have you actually addressed the requirement? If the question says for example, 'discuss the issues to be considered when switching to ZBB' – don't then simply describe ZBB; discuss the issues when switching!

Reading time

The CBE exam duration is of 3 hours, plus 10 minutes to read pre-exam instructions.

Quality and accuracy are of the utmost importance to us so if you spot an error in any of our products, please send an email to mykaplanreporting@kaplan.com with full details, or follow the link to the feedback form in MyKaplan.

Our Quality Co-ordinator will work with our technical team to verify the error and take action to ensure it is corrected in future editions.

A revision of Management Accounting (MA) topics

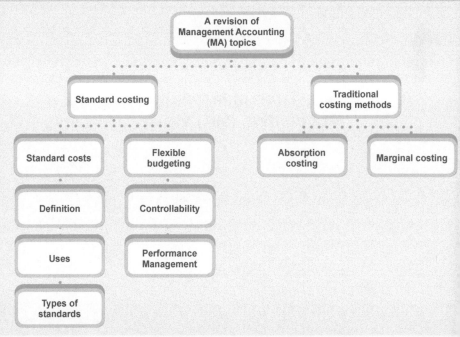

Cost definitions examples

Ideal standard	• Ideal operating conditions • Highlights cost of inefficiencies

Attainable standard	• Efficient operating conditions • Includes allowance for wastage

Current standard	• Current operating conditions • No incentive to improve efficiency

Basic standard	• Set for the long term • Highlights changes in costs

Uses of standard costing
- performance management
- inventory valuation
- setting selling prices
- budgeting
- management by exception

2

Management information systems

In this chapter

- Controls.

Information and Data

Data consists of numbers, letters, symbols, raw facts, events and transactions which have been recorded but not yet processed into a form that is suitable for making decisions.

Information is data that has been processed in such a way that it has a meaning to the person who receives it, who will then use it to improve the quality of decision-making.

Good information should be **ACCURATE**:

Accurate

Complete

Cost effective

Understandable

Relevant

Accessible

Timely

Easy to use

Information Technology (IT)

The supporting hardware that provides the infrastructure to run the information systems. It is concerned with capture, storage, transmission, or presentation of information.

Information systems (IS)

The provision and management of information to support the running of the organisation.

Privacy and security:

Privacy and security risks:

Potential threat	Potential solution
Natural disasters	Fire procedures
Malfunction	Back-up procedures
Viruses	Anti-virus software
Hackers	Firewall software
Human errors	Training
Human resource risk	Ergonomic workstation design

Controls

General controls

Ensure the organisation has overall control over its systems, e.g.:

- Personal controls
- Access controls
- Computer equipment controls
- Business continuity planning

Application or program controls

Performed automatically by the system e.g.:

- Completeness checks
- Validity checks
- Identification and authorisation checks
- Problem management facilities

Confidential / sensitive information

Controls will be required when generating and distributing confidential information.

Type of control	Explanation	Example
Input	Inputs should be complete, accurate and authorised.	Passwords
Processing	Processing should be initiated by appropriate personnel and logs should be kept of any processing.	Audit trails
Output	The output should be available to authorised persons and third parties only.	Distribution lists

Data visualisation allows large volumes of complex data to be displayed in a visually appealing and accessible way that facilitates the understanding and use of the underlying data.

Features and key benefits

5 features of effective data visualisation:

- Aids decision making.
- Effective infrastructure ensuring quality of data.
- Integration with existing systems.
- Live data.
- Real-time collaboration between users.

Key benefits

- Accessible – user friendly and intuitive.
- Real time – quick response to changes.
- Performance optimisation – proactive, efficient utilisation of resources.
- Insight and understanding – about cause and effect relationships.

Reports for decision-making

Modern reports needed to be tailored to the user or division. They should:

- be **personalised** to ensure optimal understanding
- be **interactive** where necessary
- have a **delivery channel which is optimised** to the way in which the reports will be viewed.

Tools for report visualisation:

- Dashboards
- Waterfall charts/bridges
- Line charts
- Mapping charts
- Pie charts

3

Information systems and data analytics

In this chapter

- Performance management information systems.
- Big Data.

Performance management information systems

Information requirements at different levels.

STRATEGIC PLANNING

Information predominantly environmental. Information imprecise and speculative. Long-term forecasts. Main output targets and plans. Ad hoc control system. Use decision making system such as an EIS.

MANAGEMENT CONTROL

Information concerned with efficiency and effective use of resources in the whole organisation. May involve responsibility centres. Includes measures of productivity, budget performance, labour and capacity utilisation. Use decision making system such as a DSS.

OPERATIONAL CONTROL

Short-term control information.
Very detailed.
May be in terms of quantity, rates and times rather than finance. Use decision making system such as a TPS.

Decision based systems

Management information system (MIS)
A MIS converts internal and external data into useful information which is then communicated to managers at all levels and across all functions to enable them to make timely and effective decisions.

Executive information system (EIS)
An EIS gives senior executives access to internal and external information. Information is presented in a user-friendly, summarised form with an option to 'drill down' to a greater level of detail.

Transaction processing system (TPS)
A TPS (or data processing system) processes routine business transactions, often in large volumes. For example, sales and purchase information.

Enterprise resource planning system (ERPS)
An ERPS integrates the data from all operations within the organisation into one single system. It ensures everyone is working off the same system, and includes decision support features to assist management with decision making.

Customer relationship management system (CRM)
CRM is an approach to build and sustain long term business with customers. It consists of the processes a company uses the track and organise its contacts with its current and prospective customers.

Big Data

Big Data refers to extremely large collections of data that may be analysed to reveal patterns, trends and associations.

Analysing big data is made difficult due to the following characteristics of big data:

- Velocity
- Volume
- Variety
- Veracity
- Value

Big Data Analysis is the process of scrutinising Big Data to identify patterns, correlations, relationships and other insights.

Hadoop is an open source programming framework which enables the processing of large data sets by utilising multiple servers simultaneously.

The big data pyramid

A model representing structural and functional relationships between data, information, knowledge, and wisdom:

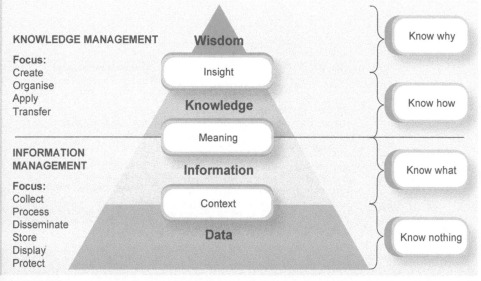

Each step up the pyramid answers questions about, and adds value to, the initial data:

WISDOM/INSIGHT: Adjusting our business decisions. Based on how our business is growing, we will accelerate the launch of our product

The ability to apply knowledge towards particular goals

KNOWLEDGE: Some insight gained from the information provided. For example, competition around us is growing

Information applied to answer 'why' questions

INFORMATION: Facts put in context. For example, a list of addresses of new competitors that are registered in the same region/geographical area as us

Data used and contextualised as answers to 'what, who, where, when' questions

DATA: A collection of facts. For example, a collection/list of adresses

Discrete, objective facts obtained from sensors or surveys

Future

Past

Benefits of Big Data	Risks associated with Big Data
• Drives innovation. • Improved customer service and decision making. • Storage of transactional data in a digital format. • Use to develop the next generation of products or services. • Access to external information. • Can create new revenue streams. • Source of competitive advantage. • Ensures measurable outcomes.	• Skills to use systems may not exist. • Security of data. • Valuable time may be spent measuring relationships that have no organisational value. • Incorrect data may result in incorrect conclusions. • Technical difficulties integrating systems. • Cost of establishing hardware and software.

(questions from the ACCA Performance Management (PM) exam kit)

OBJECTIVE CASE QUESTIONS	CONSTRUCTED RESPONSE QUESTIONS
Silversafe	B5 cars EIS
	The MG Organisation

Specialist cost and management accounting techniques

In this chapter

- Activity Based Costing (ABC).
- Target costing.
- Value analysis.
- Lifecycle costing.
- Throughput.
- Environmental cost accounting.

Activity Based Costing (ABC)

This is a key costing method. Comparisons of ABC with traditional methods of overhead absorption are particularly important. Approach calculations by using the methodical step by step approach.

The written elements of ABC are also important. Be prepared to explain the reasons for the development of ABC, its advantages and disadvantages, and the implications of ABC.

Steps

1. Group production overheads into activities, according to how they are driven.
2. Identify cost drivers for each activity.
3. Calculate a CDR for each activity cost.
4. Absorb the activity costs into each product.
5. Calculate the production cost and the profit/(loss) if required.

Advantages

- More realistic costs.

- Better insight into cost drivers, resulting in better cost control.

- Particularly useful where overhead costs are a significant proportion of total costs.

- ABC recognises that overhead costs are not all related to production and sales volume.

- ABC can be applied to all overhead costs, not just production overheads.

- ABC can be used just as easily in service costing as in product costing.

Criticisms of ABC

- It is impossible to allocate all overhead costs to specific activities.

- The choice of both activities and cost drivers might be inappropriate.

- ABC can be more complex to explain to the stakeholders of the costing exercise.

- The benefits obtained from ABC might not justify the costs.

- ABC will be of limited benefit if overhead costs are primarily volume related or are a small proportion of the total cost.

Implications

- Pricing – more realistic costs improve cost plus pricing.

- Sales strategy – more realistic margins can help focus sales strategy.

- Decision making – e.g. research and development can be directed at products with better margins.

- Performance management can be improved due to the settings of more realistic budgets and improved cost control.

Target costing

> Estimate a market driven selling price for a new product, e.g. to capture a required market share

> Reduce this figure by the company's required level of profit

> Produce a target cost figure for product designers to meet

> Calculate the cost gap:
> Target cost gap = Estimated product cost – Target cost

> Close the cost gap. This may be done through value analysis, functional analysis or value engineering

Closing the target cost gap

- "Value analysis" looks at identifying which product features contribute to customer perceived value and which do not.

- Focus is on reducing cost without compromising perceived value.

- Can labour savings be made, e.g. by using lower skilled workers?

- Can productivity be improved, e.g. by improving motivation?

- What production volume is needed to achieve economies of scale?

- Could cost savings be made by reviewing the supply chain?

- Can any materials be eliminated, e.g. cut down on packing materials?

- Can a cheaper material be substituted without affecting quality?

- Can part-assembled components be bought in to save on assembly time?

- Can the incidence of the cost drivers be reduced?

Implications

- Pricing – will be more realistic since customer demand is considered.

- Cost control – target cost motivates managers to find new ways of saving costs.

- Performance management – enhanced because the business finds ways to reduce costs.

Value analysis

To ensure target costs can be achieved, value analysis is used. Value Analysis identifies any unnecessary cost elements within the components of goods and services.

Cost Value	Exchange Value
Use Value	Esteem Value

Lifecycle costing

A common mistake in questions is that candidates confuse lifecycle costing with the product lifecycle.

Lifecycle costing

- Is the profiling of cost over a product's life, including the pre-production stage.

- Tracks and accumulates the actual costs and revenues attributable to each product from inception to abandonment.

- Enables a product's true profitability to be determined at the end of its economic life.

$$\text{Lifecycle cost of a product} = \frac{\text{Total cost of product over its entire lifecycle}}{\text{Total number of units of the product}}$$

Background

- The commitment of a high level of costs at the earlier stages of the product lifecycle (especially pre-production) has led to the need for accounting systems that compare revenues with all costs incurred throughout the lifecycle.

- Traditional costing systems based around annual periods may give a misleading impression of costs and profitability.

Implications

- **Pricing** decisions can be based on total lifecycle costs rather than simply the costs for the current period.

- **Decision making** – In deciding to produce or purchase a product or service, a timetable of life cycle costs helps show what costs need to be allocated to a product so that an organization can recover its costs. If all costs cannot be recovered, it would not be wise to produce the product or service.

- **Performance Management (Control)**
  - Lifecycle costing thus reinforces the importance of tight control over locked-in costs, such as R&D in the development stage.

- **Performance Management (Reporting)**
  - Lifecycle costing traces R&D, design, production set-up, marketing and customer service costs to products over their entire life cycles, to aid comparison with product revenues generated in later periods.

Benefits of lifecycle costing

- Draws management attention too all costs (production and non-production).
- Measures all costs from concept to withdrawal.
- Drives cost focussed decisions at the design stage – focus on long-term sustainable products rather than short-term unsustainable gains.
- Management can make better decisions re: pricing, designs, products.

Throughput

Work through the methodical step by step approach for multi product decisions.

Background

- Application of key factor analysis to production bottlenecks.
- The only totally variable cost is the purchase cost of raw materials and components that are bought from external suppliers.
- Direct labour costs are not wholly variable.

Criticisms

- It concentrates on the short term. More difficult to apply to the longer term, when all costs are variable.
- In the longer term as activity based costing might be more appropriate for measuring and controlling performance.

Multi-product decisions

Steps:

1 Determine the limiting factor (bottleneck resource).

2 For each product calculate the throughput per unit (revenue – raw material cost).

3 For each product calculate the throughput per unit of the limiting factor.

4 Rank in order.

5 Production plan – using the ranking allocate the scarce resources in the optimum way.

The throughput accounting ratio (TPAR)

$$\text{Throughput accounting ratio} = \frac{\text{Throughput per hour of bottleneck resource}}{\text{Operating expenses per hour of bottleneck resource}}$$

How to improve the TPAR

- Increase the sales price for each unit sold, to increase the throughput per unit.

- Reduce total operating expenses, to reduce the cost per assembly hour.

- Improve productivity, reducing the time required to make each unit of product.

Throughput accounting and the Theory of Constraints is the subject of two technical articles published by the examiner on the ACCA website.

Theory of constraints

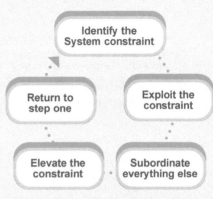

Identify the System constraint

Exploit the constraint

Subordinate everything else

Elevate the constraint

Return to step one

Environmental cost accounting

Environmental costs

Internal costs directly impact on the income statement of a company

External costs are imposed on society at large but not borne by the company that generates the cost in the first instance

Improved systems

waste disposal costs

product take back costs

regulatory costs

upfront costs

backend costs

carbon emissions

usage of energy and water

forest degradation

health care costs

social welfare costs

EMA

- The identification, collection, analysis and use of two types of information for internal decision making:
  - Physical information on the use, flows and destinies of energy, water and materials (including wastes).
  - Monetary information on environment-related costs, earnings and savings.

Environmental costs

- Waste.
- Water.
- Energy.
- Transport and travel.
- Consumables and raw materials.

Internal reporting

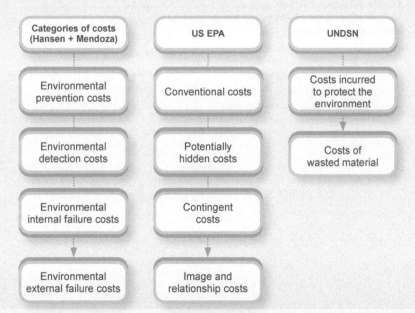

Environmental management accounting techniques

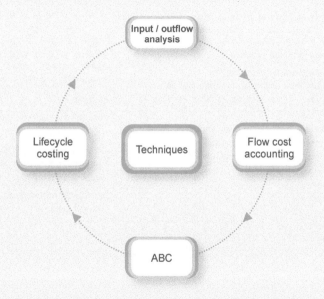

Enviromental and sustainability factors

Sustainability can be thought of as an attempt to provide the best outcomes for the human and natural environments, both now and into the indefinite future:

- Inputs (resources) must only be consumed at a rate at which they can be reproduced, offset or in some other way not irreplaceably depleted.

- Outputs (such as waste and products) must not pollute the environment at a rate greater than can be cleared or offset.

The role of a management accountant

They will apply their skills and competencies to help develop **sustainable strategies** that are more **forward looking**, about **value creation** and **risk mitigation** and are not focused on unsustainable behaviour such as short-termism or adverse resource usage.

This can include:

- Creating an ethics-based culture

- Championing sustainability

- Risk management around sustainable and environmental factors

- Performance management focused on sustainable and environmental measures.

Triple bottom line reporting

TBL reporting expands the traditional company reporting framework to take into account environmental and social performance in addition to financial (economic) performance, by looking at the following 3 headings:

	Focus	Typical measures
Planet	reduce 'ecological footprint' by managing resource consumption, energy usage and limiting environmental damage.	• Electricity/fuel consumption • Water usage • Pollutants produced • % of resources recycled
People	'social performance' for workers and surrounding community.	• Jobs created • Average pay levels • Health & Safety measures • Equality/diversity measures
Profit	'economic performance' balanced with the other two objectives.	• Profitability • Taxes paid

(questions from the ACCA Performance Management (PM) exam kit)

OBJECTIVE CASE QUESTIONS	CONSTRUCTED RESPONSE QUESTIONS
Duff Co (June 2014)	
Beckley Hill (June 2015)	
Abkaber Plc	
Chemical Free Clean Co (December 2015)	
Darask Co (Sept/Dec 2021)	
Midhurst (Sept/Dec 2020)	
Yam Co	
Brick By Brick	

5

Cost volume profit analysis

In this chapter

- Breakeven/CVP analysis.
- Basic breakeven chart.
- Contribution breakeven chart.

Breakeven/CVP analysis

Contribution = Sales price – Variable costs

$$\text{Breakeven point} = \frac{\text{Fixed costs}}{\text{Contribution per unit}}$$

$$\text{Breakeven sales revenue} = \frac{\text{Fixed costs}}{\text{Contribution to sales ratio}}$$

$$\text{Output required for target profit} = \frac{\text{Fixed cost} + \text{Target profit}}{\text{Unit contribution}}$$

$$\text{Sales revenue required for target profit} = \frac{\text{Target Profit} + \text{Fixed costs}}{\text{Contribution to sales ratio}}$$

Margin of safety = Budgeted level of activity – Breakeven level of activity

$$\text{Margin of safety (\%)} = \frac{\text{Budgeted level of activity} - \text{Breakeven level of activity}}{\text{Budgeted level of activity}} \times 100\%$$

Basic breakeven chart

Breakeven analysis – break-even chart

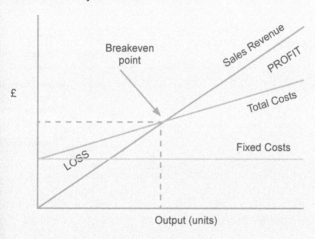

Breakeven point:
the point where
total costs = total sales revenue
and
Where there is **neither a profit or loss**

The diagram is known as the break-even chart.

Contribution breakeven chart

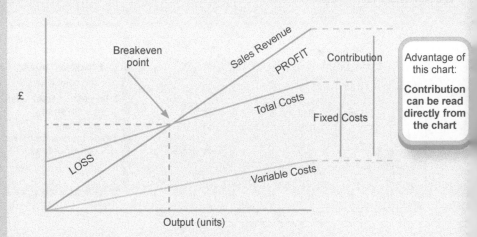

The diagram is known as the **contribution break-even chart.**

Multi-product breakeven analysis

The calculation of breakeven point in a multi-product firm follows the same pattern as in a single product firm. While the numerator will be the same fixed costs, the denominator now will be the **weighted average contribution margin**.

In multi-product situations, a weighted average C/S ratio is calculated by using the formula:

$$\text{Weighted Average C/S ratio} = \frac{\text{Total Contribution}}{\text{Total Revenue}}$$

The Weighted Average C/S ratio is useful in its own right, as it tells us what percentage each $ of sales revenue contributes towards fixed costs; it is also invaluable in helping us to quickly calculate the breakeven point in sales revenue:

$$\text{Breakeven revenue} = \frac{\text{Fixed costs}}{\text{Weighted Average C/S ratio}}$$

Step 1 : Calculate the C/S ratio of each product being sold, and rank the products in order of profitability.

Step 2 : Draw the graph, showing cumulative sales on the x-axis.

Step 3 : Draw the line that represents the profit earned by product X.

Step 4 : Draw the line that represents the profit earned by product y, which has a lower contribution per unit than product X.

Step 5 : Draw the line joining the first and last points: it reflects the average profitability of the three products, and each point on that line represents the profit earned for the associated output, assuming that the three products are sold in the standard product mix, i.e. the mix implied in the construction of the chart.

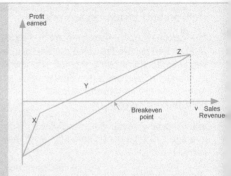

Exam focus

(questions from the ACCA Performance Management (PM) exam kit)

OBJECTIVE CASE QUESTIONS	CONSTRUCTED RESPONSE QUESTIONS
Cardio Co (December 2015)	Chocolates Are Forever
Hare Events (December 2016	Mango Leather
	Breakeven
	EC Ltd
	Health Nuts (Deptember/September 2020)

6

Planning with limiting factors

In this chapter

- Limiting factor analysis.
- Linear programming.

Limiting factor analysis

A limiting factor is a factor of production that is in **short supply** to the extent that sales demand cannot be met. Under these circumstances the approach is to maximise the **contribution per unit of limiting factor**.

The 5-step approach:

Step 1: Identify the limiting factor (e.g. labour, material, machine hours)

Step 2: Calculate the contribution per unit of limiting factor

Step 3: Rank the products

Step 4: Calculate the optimum production plan

Step 5: Calculate the profit (if required)

Linear programming

This is an important topic. The examiner will expect a good grasp of the step by step approach. Be ready to explain the meaning and carry out calculations for shadow prices and slack.

Linear programming is used to establish an optimum product mix when there are two or more resource constraints. This mix will achieve a certain (given) objective. The objective is usually to maximise contribution, but on occasion it is to maximise costs.

1 Define variables

e.g. "Let x = the number of tables made each month".

2 Define the objective.

e.g. "Maximise contribution, $C = 3x + 5y$".

3 Set out constraints

Non-negativity "$x \geq 0$, $y \geq 0$"

Others – e.g. "$5x + 2y \leq 20$".

4 Draw graph showing constraints and identify the feasible region.

* Get end-points of constraint lines – e.g. $5x + 2y = 20$ has end points $(4,0)$, $(0,10)$.

* Decide on scale and draw lines using end-points.

* Feasible region is below a line if constraint is "$\leq$" and above the line if "$\geq$".

5 Solve the optimal production plan – draw an example iso-contribution line by making up a suitable value of C. Move this out away from the origin to identify the optimal point – it should be the last point you get to that is still feasible.

Note: if the objective is to minimise costs, then an iso-cost line will need to be moved towards the origin.

Determine the optimal solution exactly by solving simultaneously the equations of the two lines that cross at the optimal point identified on the graph.

- Scale up one or both equations until they have the same number of "y" (or "x").

- Look at difference between the two (adjusted) equations and solve for "x" (or "y", as appropriate).

- Substitute the value of "x" (or "y") back into either of the two critical constraint equations and solve for "y" (or "x").

6 Answer the question!

- Calculate the maximum contribution / minimum cost.

- Write a recommendation to management.

Note: step 5 can be replaced with the following:

Determine the coordinates of each of the corners of the feasible region using simultaneous equations.

For each of the corners calculate the contribution and select the corner with the highest contribution.

Assumptions

Assumption	Reality
• A single quantifiable objective exists e.g. to maximise contribution.	• Multiple objectives (e.g. risk, return).
	• Learning effects.
• Each product always uses the same quantity of the scarce resources per unit.	• The selling price may have to be lowered to sell more.
• The contribution per unit is constant.	• Discounts as the quantity of materials needed increases.
	• Economies of scale.
	• Customers may expect to buy both products together.
• Products are independent – e.g. sell A not B.	• The products may be manufactured jointly together.
• The scenario is short term.	• In the long term constraints can be changed and fixed costs should be included.

Slack

- Slack is the amount by which a resource is under utilised. It will occur when the optimum point does not fall on the given resource line.

Shadow (or dual) prices

- The shadow price of a resource is the increase in value (usually extra contribution) that would result from having one extra unit of a limiting resource.

- It therefore represents the maximum premium (i.e. over the normal cost) that the firm should be willing to pay for one extra unit of each constraint.

- Non-critical constraints will have zero shadow prices as slack exists already.

- The simplest way to calculate shadow prices for a critical constraint is as follows:

Step 1: Add one unit to the constraint concerned, while leaving the other critical constraint unchanged.

Step 2: solve the revised simultaneous equations to derive a new optimal solution.

Step 3: calculate the revised optimal contribution. The increase is the shadow price for the constraint under consideration.

Exam focus

(questions from the ACCA Performance Management (PM) exam kit)

OBJECTIVE CASE QUESTIONS	CONSTRUCTED RESPONSE QUESTIONS
Cara Co (March 2019)	Cosmetics Co (December 2010)
Home electrics (March/June 2021)	Cut and Stitch (June 2010)
	CSC Co (September 2016)

7

Pricing

In this chapter

- Factors to consider when pricing (The 3 C's).
- Calculation aspects.
- Pricing approaches.
- Marketing-based approaches.

Factors to consider when pricing (The 3 C's)

Costs

- Need to cover costs to make a profit.
- May need to consider whole product portfolio (e.g. some products may be loss leaders).
- In the short term, may be happy just to cover variable costs to make some contribution.
- May need to consider whole lifecycle.

Competitors

- We need to be competitive.
- How close a substitute are competitors' products?

Customers

- How much are they willing to pay? (Need to do market research).

- Consider power of customers to go elsewhere; pressurise you to drop prices.

Calculation aspects

Price elasticity of demand (PED)

- PED = % change in demand / % change in price.
- PED >1 (elastic) ⇔ revenue increases if the price is cut.
- PED <1 (inelastic) ⇔ revenue increases if the price is raised.

Pricing approaches

Demand-based approach

Algebraic approach

- Profit maximised when MR = MC
- $MR = a - 2bQ$
- $P = a - bQ$
- 'a' is the price at which demand falls to (
- 'b' = gradient = Change in price / Chang in demand.

Tabular approach

	$	$	$	$	$	$
Price per unit	22	20	19	18	17	15
Variable cost per unit	6	6	6	6	6	6
Contribution per unit	16	14	13	12	11	9
Number of units sold	50,000	60,000	70,000	80,000	90,000	90,000
Total Contribution, in $000	800	840	910	960	990	810
Less Fixed costs, in $000	200	200	280	280	360	360
Net Profit in $000	600	640	630	680	630	450

Cost plus pricing

- Establish cost per unit – options include MC, full cost, prime cost.

- Calculate price using target mark-up or margin.

- Often used as a starting point even when using other methods.

Advantages	Disadvantages
• Widely used and accepted.	• Ignores the economic relationship between price and demand.
• Simple to calculate if costs are known.	• No attempt to establish optimum price.
• Selling price decision may be delegated to junior management.	• Different absorption methods give rise to different costs and hence different selling prices.
• Justification for price increases.	• Does not guarantee profit – if sales volumes are low fixed costs may not be recovered.
• May encourage price stability – if all competitors have similar cost structures and use similar mark-up.	• Must decide whether to use full cost, manufacturing cost or marginal cost.
	• This structured method fails to recognise the manager's need for flexibility in pricing.
	• Circular reasoning – price changes affect volume which affect unit fixed costs which affect price.

Marketing-based approaches

Price skimming

- Set a high initial price to 'skim off' customers who are willing to pay extra. Prices fall over time.

Suitability

- Little effective competition (e.g. where the product is new and different or where barriers to entry deter competition).
- A firm with liquidity problems may use market skimming to generate high cash flows early on.
- Where high prices in the early stages of a product's life might generate high initial cash flows.
- Where products have a short life cycle.

Penetration pricing

- Set a low initial price to gain market share. If a high volume is achieved, the low price could be sustainable.

Suitability

- If a firm wishes to increase market share.
- If the firm wishes to discourage new entrants from entering the market.
- If the firm wishes to shorten the initial period of the product's life cycle.
- If there are significant economies of scale to be achieved from high-volume output.
- Demand is highly elastic and so would respond well to low prices.

Linking pricing decisions for different products

- Basic idea: product A is cheap to attract customers who then also buy the higher margin product B.

- Key issue is the extent to which customer must buy the other products.

Suitability

- Complementary products.
- Product line pricing.

Volume discounts

- Discount for individual large order.
- Cumulative quantity discounts.

Suitability

- To increase customer loyalty.
- To attract new customers.
- To reduce sales processing costs.
- To Lower customer's purchasing costs.
- Clearance of surplus stock.
- Increased use of off peak capacity.

Price discrimination

- Have different prices in different markets for the same product.

Suitability

- The seller has some degree of monopoly power.
- Customers can be segregated into different markets.
- Barriers exist (or can be created) to prevent transfer between markets.
- Different elasticity in each market (set higher prices in the more inelastic segment).

Relevant cost pricing

- Price = net incremental cash flow.

Suitability

- One-off projects.

(questions from the ACCA Performance Management (PM) exam kit)

OBJECTIVE CASE QUESTIONS	CONSTRUCTED RESPONSE QUESTIONS
ALG Co (June 2015)	HS equation (December 2009)
	MKL
	Sniff Co

8

Relevant costing

In this chapter

- Relevant costing principles.
- Make v buy decisions.
- Shut down decisions.
- Joint products – the further processing decision.

Relevant costing principles

A common mistake in the exam is that candidates include irrelevant costs, e.g. sunk costs in their decision. Ensure that you understand the meaning of a 'relevant cash flow'.

In addition to the calculations, be prepared to explain the qualitative factors involved in the decision making process.

- Include future incremental cash flows arising as a direct result of the decision.

Cash   Future   Incremental

Include	Exclude
• Incremental costs.	• Depreciation.
• Opportunity costs – look at the next best alternative use of an asset foregone.	• Sunk costs.
	• Unavoidable costs.
• Incremental fixed overheads – look at whole organisation.	• Apportioned fixed overheads.
	• Financing cash flows (e.g. interest).

One off contracts

Minimum contract price = total net revelant cash flow associated with the contract.

At the minimum price, this will be a no gain, no loss contract, so any price higher than th leaves the organisation better off.

Make v buy decisions

Decision

- Look at future incremental cash flows.

- Watch out for opportunity costs – especially whether or not spare capacity exists and alternative uses for capacity.

Make or buy decisions with a limiting factor

Step 1: Calculate saving per unit of producing in house: Saving = external purchase price – VC to make.

Step 2: Work out the saving per unit of the limiting factor used by the product.

Step 3: Rank the products by the highest saving per unit of limiting factor.

Step 4: Allocate the scarce resource as per the ranking order until fully used up.

Step 5: Any products with unsatisfied demand can be satisfied by buying externally.

Practical factors

- Can the external supplier deliver sufficient quantity and quality as and when needed?

- Control of quality and delivery.

- The external supplier may possess specialist skills.

- Social factors, e.g. outsourcing may result in redundancies.

- Legal factors, e.g. outsourcing may impact contractual obligations.

- Alternative use of resources.

- Customer perception – customers may value products being made in-house.

- Confidentiality – buying in gives other companies some information about how the product is made.

Shut down decisions

Decision

- Look at future incremental cash flows.
- Apportioned overheads not relevant – only include specific incremental costs.
- Closure costs – e.g. penalties, redundancies.
- Reorganisation costs.
- Alternative uses for resources – e.g. make an alternative product?

Practical factors

- There may be additional costs, e.g. reorganisation costs which are unquantifiable at present.
- Impact on customers – e.g. expect a wide portfolio of products.
- Impact on other products – e.g. may be a loss leader.

Joint products – the further processing decision

Decision

- Look at future incremental cash flows: sell at split off v process further and then sell.
- Pre-separation ("joint") costs not relevant – only include post split-off aspects.

Exam focus

(questions from the ACCA Performance Management (PM) exam kit)

OBJECTIVE CASE QUESTIONS	CONSTRUCTED RESPONSE QUESTIONS
SIP Co	Bits and Pieces (June 2009)
Horngren Co (March/June 2022)	Stay Clean (December 2009)
	Choice of contracts

9

Risk and uncertainty

In this chapter

- Basic concepts.
- Research techniques.
- Simulation.
- Expected values.
- Sensitivity.
- Payoff tables.
- Decision trees.

Be prepared to discuss all of the techniques available for managing risk and to carry out relevant calculations.

Basic concepts

- All businesses face risk.
- Risk = variability in future returns.
- Some writers distinguish between "risk" and "uncertainty":
    - "risk" is used where it is possible to assign probabilities to the different possible outcomes
    - "uncertainty" is used where this is not possible.

- There are a number of methods available to manage risk:
    - research techniques
    - simulation
    - expected values
    - sensitivity analysis
    - maximax, maximin, minimax regret.

Research techniques

Desk research

- Information is collected from secondary sources, e.g. press articles.
- It is cheap and quick.
- However, it may not be accurate, up to date or relevant.

Field Research

- Information is collected from primary sources.
- Two sub-types:
  - Motivational research which is used to understand what factors motivate consumers to buy/not buy a product.
  - Measurement research which is used to quantify these factors, e.g. questionnaires.

Focus Groups

- Involves a small group discussion, e.g. regarding a new product.

Simulation

1 Apply probabilities to key factors in scenario analysis.

2 Use random numbers to select a particular scenario and calculate outcome.

3 Repeat until build up a picture of possible outcomes (i.e. a probability distribution).

4 Make decision based on attitude to risk.

Expected values

- EV = ∑ outcome × probability.
- Make decision based on best EV.

Advantages	Disadvantages
• Calculations are relatively simple.	• The probabilities used are usually very subjective.
• Takes risk into account.	• The EV is the average payoff if the project is repeated many times. Not useful for one-off decisions.
• Information is reduced to a single number resulting in easier decisions.	• The EV gives no indication of the dispersion of possible outcomes about the expected value. The dispersion gives information about the risk.
	• The EV may not correspond to any of the actual outcomes.

Sensitivity

- Identify key variables by calculating how much an estimate can change before the decision reverses.

- Can only vary one estimate at a time.

Payoff tables

- Prepare table of profits based on different decision choices and different possible scenarios.

- Four different ways of making a decision.

1 Expected values

- EV approach chooses the decision that gives the highest EV. Of these four methods, it is the only one to take the probabilities of the different outcomes into account.

2 Maximax

- The "optimist" chooses the decision with most attractive upside potential.

3 Maximin

- The "pessimist" limits the downside potential by choosing the decision with the most attractive "worse-case scenario".

4 Minimax regret

- Prepare a regret table.

- For each possible cell in the table, regret = actual profit compared with possible profit if had made the best decision.

- The "sore loser" chooses the decision that minimises their maximum possible regret.

Decision trees

A decision tree is a diagrammatic representation of a multi-decision problem, where all possible courses of action are represented, and every possible outcome of each course of action is shown.

Decision trees should be used where a problem involves a series of decisions being made and several outcomes arise during the decision-making process. Decision trees force the decision maker to consider the logical sequence of events. A complex problem is broken down into smaller, easier to handle sections.

The financial outcomes and probabilities are shown separately, and the decision tree is 'rolled back' by calculating expected values and making decisions.

Three step method

Step 1: Draw the tree from left to right, showing appropriate decisions and events / outcomes.

Some common symbols can be used: a square is used to represent a decision point (i.e. where a choice between different courses of action must be taken. A circle is used to represent a chance point. The branches coming away from a circle with have probabilities attached to them. All probabilities should add up to '1'.

Label the tree and relevant cash inflows/outflows and probabilities associated with outcomes.

Step 2: Evaluate the tree from right to left carrying out these two actions:

    (a) Calculate an EV at each outcome point.

    (b) Choose the best option at each decision point.

Step 3: Recommend a course of action to management.

The value of perfect information

Perfect information is when the forecast of the future outcome is always a correct prediction so the company can use it to undertake the most beneficial course of action.

Imperfect information is when the information is usually correct, but can be incorrect, so it is not as:

Value of information = Expected profit WITH the information – expected profit WITHOUT the information

(questions from the ACCA Performance Management (PM) exam kit)

OBJECTIVE CASE QUESTIONS	CONSTRUCTED RESPONSE QUESTIONS
Gam Co (June 2014)	Recyc
Mylo (September 2016)	Amelie
	Keytone Co (September/December 2022)

10

Budgeting

In this chapter

- The purposes of budgets.
- Behavioural aspects of budgeting.
- Conflicting objectives.
- Participation – top down v bottom up.
- Incremental budgeting.
- Zero based budgeting.
- Rolling budgets.
- Activity based budgeting/costing.
- Feed forward control.
- Selecting a budgetary system.
- Incorporating risk and uncertainty.
- Beyond budgeting.

The purpose of budgets

Aims

- Forecasting
- Planning
- Control
- Communication
- Co-ordination
- Evaluation
- Motivation
- Authorisation
- Delegation

The Performance Hierarchy

- Strategic planning is long term, looks at the whole organisation and defines resource requirements.

- Tactical planning is medium term, looks at the department / divisional level and specifies how to use resources.

- Operational planning is very short term, very detailed and is mainly concerned with control. Most budgeting activities fall within operational planning and control.

74

Behavioural aspects of budgeting

Key issues

- Dysfunctional behaviour – want goal congruence.

- Budgetary slack.

Management styles (Hopwood)

- Budget constrained – short-term pressure to hit budget.

- Profit conscious – emphasis on longer term company-wide performance.

- Non-accounting – emphasis on non financial aspects.

Target setting and motivation

- An expectations budget is a budget set at current achievable levels. This is unlikely to motivate managers to improve but may give more accurate forecasts for resource planning.

- An aspirations budget is a budget set at a level which exceeds the current level achieved. This will motivate managers to improve if it is seen as attainable but may always result in an adverse variance if it is too difficult to achieve. This must be managed carefully.

- For motivation purposes, an aspirations target should be set slightly above the anticipated performance level.

Conflicting objectives

- Company v division (see later).
- Division v division.
- Short-termism.
- Individualism.

Be prepared to discuss the appropriateness of the different types of budgeting and to evaluate the pros and cons of each budgeting technique.

Participation – top-down v bottom up

Advantages of participative budgets	Disadvantages of participative budgets

Advantages of participative budgets

- Increased motivation.
- Should contain better information, especially in a fast-moving or diverse business.
- Increases managers' understanding and commitment.
- Better communication.
- Senior managers can concentrate on strategy.

Disadvantages of participative budgets

- Senior managers may resent loss of control.
- Bad decisions from inexperienced managers.
- Budgets may not be in line with corporate objectives (dysfunctional behaviour).
- Budget preparation is slower and disputes can arise.
- Figures may be subject to bias if junior managers either try to impress or set easily achievable targets (budgetary slack).

Incremental budgeting

- Start with the previous period's budget or actual results and add (or subtract) an incremental amount to cover inflation and other known changes.

- Suitable for stable businesses where costs are not expected to change significantly. There should be good cost control and limited discretionary costs.

Advantages	Disadvantages
• Quickest and easiest method.	• Builds in previous problems and inefficiencies.
• Assuming that the historic figures are acceptable, only the increment needs to be justified.	• Uneconomic activities may be continued
	• Managers may spend unnecessarily to ensure they get the same (or a larger) budget next year.

Zero based budgeting

- Preparing a budget from a zero base, as though there is no expectation of current activities to continue from one period to the next, and justifying every piece of expenditure.

   1 Identify all possible services (and levels of service) and then cost each service or level of service; these are known individually as **decision packages**.

   2 Rank the decision packages in order of importance.

   3 Identify the level of funding that will be allocated to the department.

   4 Use up the funds in order of the ranking until exhausted.

- Used for allocating resources when spend is discretionary (e.g. service industry) or in public sector organisations.

Advantages	Disadvantages
• Eliminates past errors that may be perpetuated in an incremental analysis.	• Emphasises short term benefits to the detriment of long term goals.
• A considered allocation of resources.	• Budgeting can be too rigid and opportunities may not be embraced.
• Leads to increased staff involvement.	• Management skills required may not be present.
• Responds to changes in the business environment.	• Managers may feel demotivated due to the time consuming process.
• Knowledge and understanding of the cost behaviour patterns of the organisation will be enhanced.	• Ranking activities difficult.

Rolling budgets

- A budget kept continuously up to date by adding another accounting period (eg month or quarter) when the earliest accounting period has expired.

- Aim: to keep tight control and always have an accurate budget for the next 12 months.

- Suitable if accurate forecasts cannot be made, or for any area of business that needs tight control.

Activity based budgeting/ costing

- Use ABC for budgeting purposes:

  Step 1 Identify cost pools and cost drivers.

  Step 2 Calculate a budgeted cost driver rate based on budgeted cost and budgeted activity.

  Step 3 Produce a budget for each department or product by multiplying the budgeted cost driver rate by the expected usage.

Advantages	Disadvantages
• Greater focus on understanding overheads.	• Extra time and effort to establish an ABB system.
• Greater control of overheads.	• Problems linking ABB activities to established responsibility centres.
• Can be useful in a TQM environment, relating costs to quality.	• In the short term many overheads are not controllable and do not vary directly with changes in the volume of activity for the cost driver.

Feed forward control

- Feed-forward control is defined as the 'forecasting of differences between actual and planned outcomes and the implementation of actions before the event, to avoid such differences.

- In simpler terms, feedforward control is where a problem is identified and corrective action taken, before the problem occurs.

- An example would be using a cash-flow budget to forecast a funding problem and as a result arranging a higher overdraft well in advance of the problem.

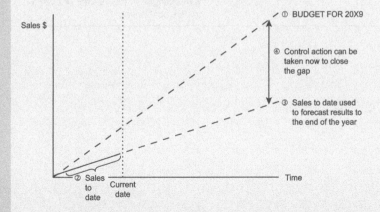

Advantages	Disadvantages
• It encourages managers to be pro active and deal with problems before they occur.	• It may be time consuming as control reports must be produced regularly.
• Re-forecasting on a monthly or continuous basis can save time when it comes to completing a quarterly or annual budget.	• It may require a sophisticated forecasting system, which might be expensive.

Selecting a budgetary system

Determinants

* Type of organisation.
* Type of industry.
* Type of product and product range.
* Culture of the organisation.

Factors to consider when changing a budgetary system

* Are suitably trained staff are available to implement the change successfully?
* Will changing the system take up management time which should be focusing on production or sales?
* All staff involved in the budgetary process will need to be trained.
* Cost v benefits for the new system:
  - Costs include new system costs, training, downtime of existing staff, consultancy fees and development of new statistical models and sources of information suitable for the new budgetary system.
  - Benefits may be difficult to quantify.
* As a result organisations may (often!) persevere with a sub-optimal system.

Incorporating risk and uncertainty

* Rolling budgets.
* Simulation.
* Sensitivity analysis.

Beyond budgeting

	Traditional Budgeting Management Model	Beyond Budgeting Management Model
Targets & rewards	Incremental targets Fixed incentives	Stretch goals Relative targets & rewards
Planning & controls	Fixed annual plans Variance controls	Continuous planning KPI's & rolling forecasts
Resource & coordination	Pre-allocated resources Central co-ordination	Resources on demand Dynamic coordination
Organisational culture	Central control Focus on managing numbers	Local control of goals/plans Focus on value creation

(questions from the ACCA Performance Management (PM) exam kit)

OBJECTIVE CASE QUESTIONS	CONSTRUCTED RESPONSE QUESTIONS
LRA (June 2015)	Static Co (December 2016)
Corfe Co (September 2016)	NN
	Zero-based budgeting
	Yumi (Spetember 2019)

Quantitative techniques

In this chapter

- High-low.
- Learning curves.
- Linear regression.
- Time series analysis.

High-low

- Used to determine a linear relationship between two variables – usually to split costs into fixed and variable elements.

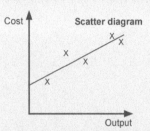

Cost

Scatter diagram

Output

- Step 1: Select the highest and lowest activity levels, and their costs.

- Step 2: Find the variable cost/unit.

$$\text{Variable cost/unit} = \frac{\text{Cost at high level activity} - \text{Cost at low level activity}}{\text{High level of activity} - \text{Low level of activity}}$$

- Step 3: Find the fixed cost, using either the high or low activity level.

  Fixed cost = Total cost at activity level – Total variable cost.

- Step 4: Use the variable and fixed cost to forecast the total cost for a specified level of activity.

Learning curves

This is an important topic. The technique is similar for all questions and therefore practice is the key to scoring a good mark. Be prepared to discuss the implications of the learning curve effect and the conditions required for the learning effect to apply.

Mechanics

*   As cumulative output doubles, the cumulative average time per unit falls to a fixed % (the learning rate) of the previous average.

$$y = ax^b$$

where y = average time (or average cost) per unit or per batch

a = time (or cost) for first unit or per batch

$b = \dfrac{\log r}{\log 2}$ (r = rate of learning)

x = cumulative output in units or in batches

*   Key issue is to see units as part of the history of production (e.g. units have serial numbers).

    E.g. time to make 20th item = total time to make first 20 units – time to make first 19 units.

Conditions for the learning effect to apply:

- The activity is labour intensive and relatively complex so that learning can occur.
- A repetitive process for each unit.
- The product is new.
- The product is complex.
- Early stages of production.
- No prolonged breaks in production.

Cessation of the learning effect (steady state):

- Machine efficiency restricts further improvements.
- 'Go slow' agreements.

Linear regression

$$a = \bar{y} - b\bar{x} = \frac{\Sigma y}{n} - \frac{b\Sigma x}{n}$$

$$b = \frac{n\Sigma xy - \Sigma x\Sigma y}{n\Sigma x^2 - (\Sigma x)^2}$$

- The symbol Σ means 'the sum of the values of'.
- n is the number of pairs of data for values of x and y that are being used to calculate the line of best fit.
- Calculate b first, than a.

Advantages and disadvantages of linear regression

Advantages	Linear regression	Disadvantages

Advantages	Disadvantages
Commonly used technique	Assumes what has happened in the past is a reliable guide to the future
Takes account of all data	Assumes the relationship is linear
Mathematically accurate estimate of the trend	The data must be strongly correlated

Time series analysis

Steps in analysing time series with seasonal trends	Definitions
Identify any underlying historical trend and measure it	A trend is an underlying long-term movement of data and may be upwards, downwards or flat.
Forecast trend into the future	Seasonal variations are the short-term variations in the measured values in the time series, above or below the trend line, due to seasonal factors. Vary according to the type of industry.
Identify any seasonal variations around trend and measure them	
Apply seasonal variation to trend line to forecast season by season	

Advantages and disadvantages of time series analysis

| Advantages | Time Series Forecasting | Disadvantages |

Forecasts based on clearly understood assumptions

Reliability of forecast can be assessed as each successive period finishes

Forecasting accuracy improves with experience

Assumes what has happened in the past is a reliable guide to the future

Assumption that a straight line trend exists

Assumption that seasonal variations are constant

(questions from the ACCA Performance Management (PM) exam kit)

OBJECTIVE CASE QUESTIONS	CONSTRUCTED RESPONSE QUESTIONS
BokCo (June 2015)	Big cheese chairs (December 09)
Bellamy Co	Henry Company (December 09)
	ATD (December 2013)

12

Advanced variances

In this chapter

- Sales variances.
- Materials mix and yield variances.
- Other targets for controlling production processes.
- Planning and operational variances.
- Modern manufacturing environments.

Sales variances

Total sales variance

Sales price variance

- Calculation unchanged
- Calculate a seperate variance for each product

Sales volume variance

Sales mix variance

- Measures the impact on profit of a change in the sales mix of products sold

Sales quality variance

- Measures the impact on profit of a different total quantity of products actually sold to budgeted

Actual Quantity Sold × Actual Price	(AQ AP)	Price Variance
Actual Quantity Sold × Standard Price	(AQ SP)	
Actual Quantity Sold × Standard Margin	(AQ SM)	Volume Variance
Budget Quantity × Standard Margin	(BQ SM)	

Note: 'Margin' = contribution per unit (marginal costing) or profit per unit (absorption costing).

Materials mix and yield variances

Mix and Yield variances are examined very frequently. It may help to use a tabular approach when calculating these variances.

Be prepared to explain the meaning of each variance and the possible causes of the variances calculated.

Basic idea

- Only use where materials can be substituted for each other.

- Still do separate price variances for each material.

- Mix and yield are **instead** of separate usage variances.

```
        ┌──────────────────┐
        │  Material usage  │
        │     variance     │
        └──────────────────┘
   · · · · · · · · · · · · · · · ·
┌──────────────────┐   ┌──────────────────┐
│  Material mix    │   │  Material yield  │
│     variance     │   │     variance     │
└──────────────────┘   └──────────────────┘
```

Calculations

Actual total Q input	in actual mix	@standard prices	X	} Mix Variance
Actual total Q input	in standard mix	@standard prices	X	
Standard total Q input (for actual output)	in standard mix	@standard prices	X	} Yield Variance

Mix variance

Material	AQAM	AQSM	Difference	@ standard price	Variance
A	X	X	X	$X	$X
B	X	X	X	$X	$X
Total	X ⟶	X			$X

Yield variance

Material	AQSM	SQSM	Difference	@ standard price	Variance
A	X	X	X	$X	$X
B	X	X	X	$X	$X
Total	X ⟶	X			$X

Possible reasons

Mix – A favourable variance would suggest that a higher proportion of a cheaper material was used. This could be due to:

- A decision to cut costs.
- Greater availability of cheaper materials.
- Unavailability of other (more expensive) materials.
- Costs of other materials having risen so it was decided to use less of them.

Yield – An adverse variance would suggest that less output has been achieved for a given input, i.e. that the total input in volume is more than expected for the output achieved. This could be due to:

- labour inefficiencies
- higher waste
- inferior materials
- using a cheaper mix with a lower yield.

Other targets for controlling production processes

- Quality measures, e.g. % waste, % yield.
- Average cost of inputs.
- Average cost of output.
- Average prices achieved for finished products.
- Average margins.
- % on-time deliveries.
- Customer satisfaction ratings.
- Detailed timesheets.
- % idle time.

Mix – Actual in AM @ SP
        Actual in SM @ SP

Yield Actual in SM @ SP
        Budget in SM @ SP

Planning and operational variances

It is important to be able to calculate the variances but it is equally as important to be able to interpret each variance and discuss the reasons why a standard should be revised.

Original budget
(ex-ante)

Planning variances
(uncontrollable?)

Revised budget
(ex-post)

Operating variances
Controllable?)

Actual results

Or

Advantages	Disadvantages
• Variances are more relevant.	• The establishment of ex-post budgets is very difficult.
• The operational variances give a 'fair' reflection of the actual results achieved in the actual conditions.	• Managers whose performance is reported to be poor using such a budget are unlikely to accept them.
• Managers are more likely to accept and be motivated by the variances.	• Extra administration.
• It emphasises the importance of planning.	• The analysis tends to exaggerate the interrelationship of variances.
• The analysis helps in the standard setting learning process.	• Poor performance is often excused as being the fault of a badly set budget.
	• Frequent demands for revisions may result in bias.

Good reasons to revise standards

- A change in one of the main materials used to make a product.

- An unexpected increase in the price of materials due to a rapid increase in world market prices (e.g. the price of oil or other commodities).

- A change in working methods that alters the expected direct labour time for a product or service.

- An unexpected change in the rate of pay to the workforce.

Market size and market shares variances

- Split the sales volume variance into two elements.

Original budget sales	x standard margin	
Revised budget sales (to achieve target share of actual market	x standard margin	Market size variance (planning)
Actual sales quantity x	standard margin	Market share variance (operational)

(handwritten annotations in right margin:)

Op Plan
Planning
Size Variance
On BS × SM — planning
R BS × SM
R BS × SM — op
AS × SM

Planning and operating cost variances

- When applying planning and operating principles to cost variances, care must be taken over volumes and flexing the budgets.

- The examiner's approved approach for use in the exam is to flex both the original and revised budgets to actual production levels.

- For operational variances, the revised standards and flexed budget supersede the original standards.

Original budget
(flexed)

    Planning variances

Revised budget
(flexed)

    Operating variances

Actual results

Modern manufacturing environments

Total Quality Management (TQM)

TQM is the continuous improvement in quality, productivity and effectiveness through a management approach focusing on both process and the product.

Fundamental features include:

- recognition that quality is determined by customer requirements

- prevention of errors before they occur

- importance of total quality in the design of systems and products

- real participation of all employees

- commitment of senior management to the cause

- recognition of the need for continual improvement.

Just-in-time (JiT)

JIT is a pull-based system of planning and control.

- Pulling work through the system in response to customer demand.
- Goods are only produced when they are needed.
- This eliminates large inventories of materials and finished goods.

Key characteristics for successfully operating such a system are:

- High quality – possibly through deploying TQM systems.
- Speed: rapid throughput to meet customers' needs.
- Reliability: computer-aided manufacturing technology will assist.
- Flexibility: small batch sizes and automated techniques are used.
- Low costs: through all of the above.

Relevance of variance analysis

- Standard product costs apply to manufacturing environments in which identical products are made. They are not suitable where products are customised to customer specifications.
- Standard costs become outdated quickly in a modern business environment.
- It is doubtful whether standard costing is of much value in automated manufacturing environments.
- Standard costing and adherence to a preset standard is inconsistent with the concept of continuous improvement.
- Ideal standards are often used therefore adverse variances have a different meaning than if a current standard was used.
- Variance analysis is often carried out on an aggregate basis (total material usage variance, total labour efficiency variance and so on) but in a complex ar

constantly changing business environment more detailed information is required for effective management control.

- Variance analysis control reports tend to be made available to managers at the end of a reporting period. In the modern business environment managers need more 'real time' information about events as they occur.

(questions from the ACCA Performance Management (PM) exam kit)

OBJECTIVE CASE QUESTIONS	CONSTRUCTED RESPONSE QUESTIONS
Romeo Co (December 2016)	Glove Co (June 2016)
OBC (December 2015)	Kappa Co (September 2018)
Greyshott Co (March 2019)	Safe Soap Co (December 2014)
	Medical Temp Co (March/June 2021)

chapter 13

Performance measurement and control

In this chapter

- Overview.
- Ratio analysis.
- Non-financial performance indicators.

Overview

A key topic. Tested in detail in all exams to date.

An effective system of performance measurement is critical if investments / divisions / managers are to be controlled.

Typical measures include the following:

- profit, revenue, margins
- share price if listed
- ratio analysis
- ROI, RI for divisions
- variances
- non-financial measures (very important!).

Ratio analysis

Preliminaries

- Ratios may not be representative of the position throughout a period.
  E.g. seasonal trade.

- Need a basis for comparison.

  - Budgets, for control purposes.

  - Last year's figures to identify trends.

  - Competitors' results and/or industry averages to assess performance.

- Ratios can be manipulated by management. E.g. "window dressing".

- Ratios indicate areas for further investigation rather than giving answers.

Profitability ratios

- $ROCE = \dfrac{\text{Net Profit}}{\text{Capital Employed}} \times 100\%$

- $\text{Gross margin} = \dfrac{\text{Gross profit}}{\text{Sales}} \times 100\%$

- $\text{Net margin} = \dfrac{\text{Net profit}}{\text{Sales}} \times 100\%$

- $\text{Asset turnover} = \dfrac{\text{Sales}}{\text{Capital Employed}}$

ROCE = net margin x asset turnover

Liquidity / working capital ratios

- $\text{Current Ratio} = \dfrac{\text{Current Assets}}{\text{Current Liabilities}}$

- $\text{Quick Ratio (acid test)} = \dfrac{\text{Current Assets minus inventory}}{\text{Current liabilities}}$

- $\text{Receivables days} = \dfrac{\text{Receivables}}{\text{Credit sales}} \times 365$

- $\text{Payables days} = \dfrac{\text{Payables}}{\text{Credit purchases}} \times 365$

- $\text{Inventory days} = \dfrac{\text{Inventory}}{\text{Cost of sales}} \times 365$

Measuring risk

- $\text{Financial Gearing} = \dfrac{\text{Debt}}{\text{Equity}}$

  or $= \dfrac{\text{Debt}}{\text{Debt + Equity}}$

- $\text{Dividend Cover} = \dfrac{\text{Net Profit}}{\text{Total Dividend}}$

- $\text{Interest Cover} = \dfrac{\text{Operating Profit}}{\text{Interest}}$

Non-financial performance indicators

The examiner has stated that candidates must understand that a balance is needed between financial and non-financial performance indicators. A seemingly reasonable financial result can hide much deeper problems which, if left unchecked, can result in financial disaster.

- Financial performance appraisal often reveals the ultimate effects of operational factors and decisions but non-financial indicators are needed to monitor causes.

- The achievement of these goals is monitored using a number of measures, many of which are non-financial.

- A firm's success usually involves focussing on a small number of goals where they must win.

Stakeholders

- Different stakeholders will have different objectives. Companies may deal with this by having a range of performance measures.

The balanced scorecard
(Kaplan and Norton)

Financial perspective
How do we look to shareholders and lenders?

Customer perspective
How do customers see us?

VISION AND STRATEGY

Innovation and learning
Can we continue to improve and create value?

Internal business processes
What must we excel at?

Benefits of the balanced scorecard	Problems with the balanced scorecard
• It makes use of external as well as internal information.	• Selection of measures.
• It focuses on factors, including non financial ones, which will enable a company to succeed.	• Obtaining information.
	• Information overload.
	• Conflict between measures.

The building block model (Fitzgerald et al)

Dimensions

- Financial performance
- Competitive performance
- Quality
- Flexibility
- Resource utilisation
- Innovation

Standards	Rewards
• Ownership	• Clarity
• Achievability	• Motivation
• Equity	• Controllability

Dimensions

- Sources of goals.

Standards

- Measures.

- To ensure success it is vital that employees view standards as achievable, fair and take ownership of them.

Rewards

- To ensure that employees are motivated to meet standards, targets need to be clear and linked to controllable factors.

(questions from the ACCA Performance Management (PM) exam kit)

OBJECTIVE CASE QUESTIONS	CONSTRUCTED RESPONSE QUESTIONS
Pind Co	CIM (December 2015)
	Rotech (June 2014)
	Flag Co (December 2021)
	Best Night Co (March 2019)
	Hammock Co

14

Divisional performance measurement and transfer pricing

In this chapter

- Transfer pricing.
- Divisional performance measurement.

Transfer pricing

Objectives

- Goal congruence – divisional decisions are the correct decisions for the group.
- Performance measurement.
- Autonomy.
- Minimising global tax liability.
- To record the movement of goods and services.

Exam questions

Will often be given a TP and asked to comment. Look at the following.

- Implications for divisional performance – e.g. is a target ROI achieved?
- Resulting manager behaviour – does it give dysfunctional decision making – e.g. will a manager reject a new product that is acceptable to the company as a whole?

Rules

General rule

Optimum transfer price = Marginal cost + Opportunity cost

This is also the minimum transfer price the selling division will accept.

This general rule gives the following transfer prices in three specific scenarios that you may see in the exam:

- In a perfectly competitive market, TP = market price.
- If spare capacity exists, TP = marginal cost.
- With production constraints, TP = marginal cost + opportunity cost of not using those resources elsewhere.

Practical transfer pricing systems

Market price

- Will be seen as fair by managers.
- Does an external market exist for the component?
- Prices may be linked to volume, so which to use?
- May be more than one market price – which to use?
- Are costs of selling externally the same as for internal transfers?

Production cost + mark-up

- Marginal or full cost?
- Full cost can cause problems as TP viewed as a variable cost by the receiving division.
- Standard cost aids responsibility accounting.

Negotiation

- Look at bargaining power of different parties.

Maximum transfer price the buying division will accept

Maximum TP is lower of:

- the external purchase price (e.g. from an external supplier), and
- the net marginal revenue of selling the final product.

Where:

Net marginal revenue = Final sales price – Additional variable costs

Divisional performance measurement

Key considerations

- Manager or division?
- Type of division.

Type of division	Description	Typical measures
Cost centre	• Division incurs costs but has no revenue stream.	• Total cost and cost per unit. • Cost variances. • NFPIs related to quality, productivity and efficiency.
Profit Centre	• Division has costs and revenue. • Manager **does not** have the authority to alter the level of investment in the division.	All of the above PLUS • Total sales and market share. • Profit. • Sales variances. • Working capital ratios (depending on the division concerned). • NFPIs e.g. related to productivity, quality and customer satisfaction.
Investment centre	• Division has costs and revenue. • Manager **does** have the authority to invest in new assets or dispose of existing ones.	All of the above PLUS • ROI. • RI.

Return on Investment (ROI)

An understanding of the drawbacks of ROI is essential for the exam.

$$ROI = \frac{\text{Pre tax controllable profit}}{\text{Controllable capital employed}}$$

Advantages of ROI	Disadvantages of ROI
• Relative measure (%), therefore aids comparisons between divisions of different sizes. • Used externally (ROCE) and therefore understood by users. • Encourages good use of existing capital resources. • It can be broken down into secondary ratios for more detailed analysis.	• May lead to dysfunctional decision making e.g. a division with a current ROI of 30% would not wish to accept a project offering an ROI of 25% as this would dilute its current figure. • ROI increases as assets get older if NBVs are used, thus giving managers an incentive to hang on to possibly inefficient obsolete machines. • It may encourage the manipulation of profit and capital employed. • Different accounting policies can confuse comparisons.

Residual Income (RI)

RI = Pre tax controllable profits – imputed charge for controllable invested capital

Advantages of RI	Disadvantages of RI
• Reduces the problem of rejecting projects with ROIs greater than the group target but less than the division's current ROI.	• Does not facilitate comparisons between divisions of different sizes.
• Cost of financing a division is brought home to divisional managers.	• Profit and capital employed may be subject to manipulation.

Exam focus

(questions from the ACCA Performance Management (PM) exam kit)

OBJECTIVE CASE QUESTIONS	CONSTRUCTED RESPONSE QUESTIONS
	Mobe (June 2015)
	Division A
	Rotech (June 2014)

15

Performance measurement in not-for-profit organisations and the public sector

In this chapter

- Objectives.
- Performance measurement.

Objectives

Planning for not-for-profit organisations is usually more complex.

- Multiple objectives are more common and it may be difficult to prioritise (e.g. in a hospital, treating more patients v better quality care).

- It may be difficult to measure objectives as they are often non-financial (e.g. a charity may have the aim of reducing suffering caused by a natural disaster).

- Conflicts between stakeholders may be harder to resolve as the balance of power is more even. With companies the shareholders should 'win'.

- There are greater difficulties in measuring performance. Companies have profit as their bottom line measure.

- There are often different ways of trying to achieve the same objective – trying to choose between them can be difficult.

- Objectives may be politically driven and hence may change (e.g. government targets in education).

Performance measurement

Value for money (VFM)

- Effectiveness – Match the service provision to the need: how well are the organisation's objectives being met?

- Efficiency – Maximize the output of services for a given level of resource input.

- Economy – Source the resource input at the lowest cost.

Chapter 15

Exam focus

(questions from the ACCA Performance Management (PM) exam kit)

OBJECTIVE CASE QUESTIONS	CONSTRUCTED RESPONSE QUESTIONS
	Woodside charity (June 07)
	Robinholt University (September 2019)
	Tonford School (September/December 2020)
	Medcomp (March/June 2021)
	Wyeland (September/December 2022)

Index

R

S

T

V

Z